THE BRITISH EMPIRE

THE EMPIRE ON WHICH THE SUN NEVER SETS

CORNEL GENERAL

Contents

Contents

CHAPTER I

Introduction

The British Empire was composed of the dominions, colonies, protectorates, mandates and other territories ruled or administered by the United Kingdom and its predecessor states. It began with the overseas possessions and trading posts established by England between the late 16th and the early 18th centuries. At its height it was the largest empire in history and for over a century was the foremost global power. By 1913 the British Empire held sway over 412 million people, 23 per cent of the world population at the time and by 1920 it covered 35,500,000 km^2 (13,700,000 sq mi), 24 per cent of the Earth's total land area. As a result, its constitutional, legal, linguistic and cultural legacy is widespread. At the peak of its power, it was described as "the empire on which the sun never sets", as the sun was always shining on at least one of its territories.

During the Age of Discovery in the 15th and 16th centuries, Portugal and Spain pioneered European exploration of the globe and in the process established large overseas empires. Envious of the great wealth these empires generated England, France and the Netherlands began to establish colonies and trade networks of their own in the Americas and Asia. A series of wars in the 17th and 18th centuries with the Netherlands and France left England (Britain following the 1707 Act of Union with Scotland) the dominant colonial power in North America. Britain became the dominant power in the Indian sub-continent after the East India Company's conquest of Mughal Bengal at the

Battle of Plassey in 1757.

The American War of Independence resulted in Britain losing some of its oldest and most populous colonies in North America by 1783. British attention then turned towards Asia, Africa and the Pacific. After the defeat of France in the Napoleonic Wars (1803–1815), Britain emerged as the principal naval and imperial power of the 19th century and expanded its imperial holdings. The period of relative peace (1815–1914) during which the British Empire became the global hegemon was later described as "Pax Britannica" ("British Peace"). Alongside the formal control that Britain exerted over its colonies, its dominance of much of world trade meant that it effectively controlled the economies of many regions, such as Asia and Latin America. Increasing degrees of autonomy were granted to its white settler colonies, some of which were reclassified as Dominions.

By the start of the 20th century, Germany and the United States had begun to challenge Britain's economic lead. Military and economic tensions between Britain and Germany were major causes of the First World War, during which Britain relied heavily on its empire. The conflict placed enormous strain on its military, financial and manpower resources. Although the empire achieved its largest territorial extent immediately after World War I, Britain was no longer the world's pre-eminent industrial or military power. In the Second World War, Britain's colonies in East Asia and Southeast Asia were occupied by the Empire of Japan. Despite the final victory of Britain and its allies, the damage to British prestige helped accelerate the decline of the empire. India, Britain's most valuable and populous possession, achieved independence as part of a larger decolonisation movement, in which Britain granted independence to most territories of the empire. The Suez Crisis of 1956 confirmed Britain's decline as a global power and the transfer of Hong Kong to China on 1 July 1997 marked for many the end of the British Empire. Fourteen overseas territories remain under British sovereignty. After independence, many former British colonies joined the Commonwealth of Nations, a free association of independent states. Fifteen of these, including the United Kingdom, retain a common monarch, currently Queen Elizabeth II.

The foundations of the British Empire were laid when England and Scotland were separate kingdoms. In 1496, King Henry VII of England, following the successes of Spain and Portugal in overseas exploration, commissioned John Cabot to lead an expedition to discover a northwest passage to Asia via the North Atlantic. Cabot sailed in 1497, five years after the first voyage of Christopher Columbus, and made landfall on the coast of Newfoundland. He believed he had reached Asia, and there was no attempt to found a colony. Cabot led another voyage to the Americas the following year but he did not return from this voyage and it is unknown what happened to his ships.

No further attempts to establish English colonies in the Americas were made until well into the reign of Queen Elizabeth I, during the last decades of the 16th century. In the meantime, Henry VIII's 1533 Statute in Restraint of Appeals had declared "that this realm of England is an Empire". The Protestant Reformation turned England and Catholic Spain into implacable enemies. In 1562, Elizabeth I encouraged the privateersJohn Hawkins and Francis Drake to engage in slave-raiding attacks against Spanish and Portuguese ships off the coast of West Africa with the aim of establishing an Atlantic slave trade. This effort was rebuffed and later, as the Anglo-Spanish Wars intensified, Elizabeth I gave her blessing to further privateering raids against Spanish ports in the Americas and shipping that was returning across the Atlantic, laden with treasure from the New World. At the same time, influential writers such as Richard Hakluyt and John Dee (who was the first to use the term "British Empire") were beginning to press for the establishment of England's own empire. By this time, Spain had become the dominant power in the Americas and was exploring the Pacific Ocean, Portugal had established trading posts and forts from the coasts of Africa and Brazil to China, and France had begun to settle the Saint Lawrence River area, later to become New France.

Although England tended to trail behind Portugal, Spain, and France in establishing overseas colonies, it carried out its first modern colonisation, referred to as the Ulster Plantation, in 16th century Ireland by settling English Protestants in Ulster. England had already colonised part of the country following the Norman invasion of Ireland in 1169. Several people who helped establish the Ulster Plantations later played a part in the early colonisation of North America, particularly a group known as the West Country Men.

In 1578, Elizabeth I granted a patent to Humphrey Gilbert for discovery and overseas exploration. That year, Gilbert sailed for the Caribbean with the intention of engaging in piracy and establishing a colony in North America, but the expedition was aborted before it had crossed the Atlantic. In 1583, he embarked on a second attempt. On this occasion, he formally claimed the harbour of the island of Newfoundland, although no settlers were left behind. Gilbert did not survive the return journey to England and was succeeded by his half-brother, Walter

Raleigh, who was granted his own patent by Elizabeth in 1584. Later that year, Raleigh founded the Roanoke Colony on the coast of present-day North Carolina, but lack of supplies caused the colony to fail.

In 1603, James VI of Scotland ascended (as James I) to the English throne and in 1604 negotiated the Treaty of London, ending hostilities with Spain. Now at peace with its main rival, English attention shifted from preying on other nations' colonial infrastructures to the business of establishing its own overseas colonies. The British Empire began to take shape during the early 17th century, with the English settlement of North America and the smaller islands of the Caribbean, and the establishment of joint-stock companies, most notably the East India Company, to administer colonies and overseas trade. This period, until the loss of the Thirteen Colonies after the American War of Independence towards the end of the 18th century, has been referred to by some historians as the "First British Empire".

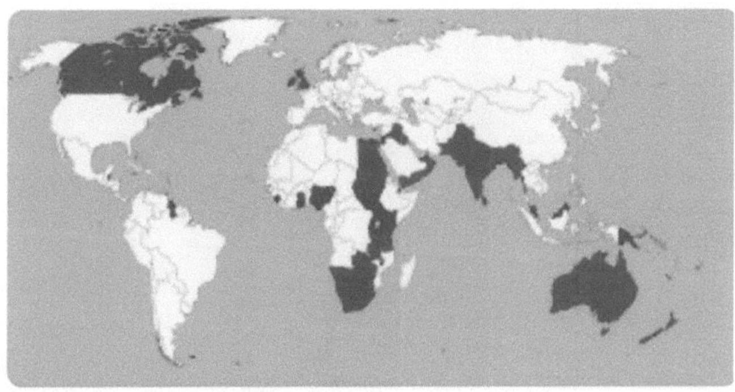

British Empire in 1919

CHAPTER II

Americas, Africa and the slave trade

England's early efforts at colonisation in the Americas met with mixed success. An attempt to establish a colony in Guiana in 1604 lasted only two years and failed in its main objective to find gold deposits. Colonies on the Caribbean islands of St Lucia (1605) and Grenada (1609) rapidly folded. The first permanent English settlement in the Americas was founded in 1607 in Jamestown by Captain John Smith, and managed by the Virginia Company; the Crown took direct control of the venture in 1624, thereby founding the Colony of Virginia. Bermuda was settled and claimed by England as a result of the 1609 shipwreck of the Virginia Company's flagship, while attempts to settle Newfoundland were largely unsuccessful. In 1620, Plymouth was founded as a haven by Puritan religious separatists, later known as the Pilgrims. Fleeing from religious persecution would become the motive for many English would-be colonists to risk the arduous trans-Atlantic voyage: Maryland was established by English Roman Catholics (1634), Rhode Island (1636) as a colony tolerant of all religions and Connecticut (1639) for Congregationalists. England's North American holdings were further expanded with the granting of a royal charter for Carolina in 1663, the annexation of the Dutch colony of New Netherland in 1664—following the surrender of Fort Amsterdam on Manhattan Island, when the colony was renamed New York—and the founding of the colony of Pennsylvania by William Penn in 1681. Although less financially successful than colonies in the Caribbean, these territories had large areas of good agricultural land and attracted far greater numbers of English emigrants, who preferred their temperate climates. The British West Indies initially provided England's most important and lucrative colonies. Settlements were successfully established in St. Kitts (1624), Barbados (1627) and Nevis (1628), but struggled until the "Sugar Revolution" transformed the Caribbean economy in the mid-17th century. Large sugarcane plantations were first established in the 1640s on Barbados, with assistance from Dutch merchants and Sephardic Jews fleeing Portuguese Brazil. At first, sugar was grown primarily using white indentured labour, but rising costs soon led English traders to enthusiastically embrace the use of imported African slaves. The enormous wealth generated by slave-produced sugar made Barbados the most successful colony in the Americas, and one of the most densely populated places in the world. This boom led to the spread of sugar cultivation across the Caribbean, financed the development of non-plantation colonies in North America, and accelerated the growth of the Atlantic slave trade, particularly the triangular trade of slaves, sugar and provisions between Africa, the West Indies and Europe.

To ensure that the increasingly healthy profits of colonial trade remained in English hands, Parliament decreed in 1651 that only English ships would be able to ply their trade in English colonies. This led to hostilities with the United Dutch Provinces—a series of Anglo-Dutch Wars—which would eventually strengthen England's position in the Americas at the expense of the Dutch. In 1655, England annexed the island of Jamaica from the Spanish, and in 1666 succeeded in colonising the Bahamas. In 1670, Charles II incorporated by royal charter the Hudson's Bay Company (HBC), granting it a monopoly on the fur trade in the area known as Rupert's Land, which would later form a large proportion of the Dominion of Canada. Forts and trading posts established by the HBC were frequently the subject of attacks by the French, who had established their own fur trading colony in adjacent New France.

Two years later, the Royal African Company was granted a monopoly on the supply of slaves to the British colonies in the Caribbean. The company would transport more slaves across the Atlantic than any other, and significantly grew England's share of the trade, from 33 per cent in 1673 to 74 per cent in 1683. The removal of this monopoly between 1688 and 1712 allowed independent British slave traders to thrive, leading to a rapid escalation in the number of slaves transported. British ships carried a third of all slaves shipped across the Atlantic—approximately 3.5 million Africans—and dominated global slave trading in the 25 years preceding its abolition by Parliament in 1807. To facilitate the shipment of slaves, forts were established on the coast of West Africa, such as James Island, Accra and Bunce Island. In the British Caribbean, the percentage of the population of African descent rose from 25 per cent in 1650 to around 80 per cent in 1780, and in the Thirteen Colonies from 10 per cent to 40 per cent over the same period (the majority in the southern colonies). The transatlantic slave trade played a pervasive role in British economic life, and became a major economic mainstay for western port cities. Ships registered in Bristol, Liverpool and London were responsible for the bulk of British slave trading. For the transported, harsh and unhygienic conditions on the slaving ships and poor diets meant that the average mortality rate during the Middle Passage was one in seven.

SLAVE TRADE
FROM AFRICA TO THE AMERICAS
1650–1860
NORTH AMERICA
U.S.
New York
Richmond
Charleston
New Orleans
Mexico City
.5 Million
.3 Million
TO EUROPE
Major Slave Trade Route
WEST INDIES
4.5 Million
CENTRAL AMERICA
.2 Million
Cartagena
Paramaribo
Pacific Ocean
SOUTH AMERICA
.5 Million
Lima
Recife
Salvador
Brazil
5 Million
Rio de Janeiro
Valparaíso
Buenos Aires
Atlantic Ocean
AFRICA
Senegal
Sierra Leone
Slave Coast
West Africa Slave Trade Regions
Congo
Angola
Tobacco
Coffee
Cotton
Sugar
Mining
Rice
Between 1650 and 1860, approximately 10 to 15 million enslaved people were transported from western Africa to the Americas. Most were shipped to the West Indies, Central America, and South America.

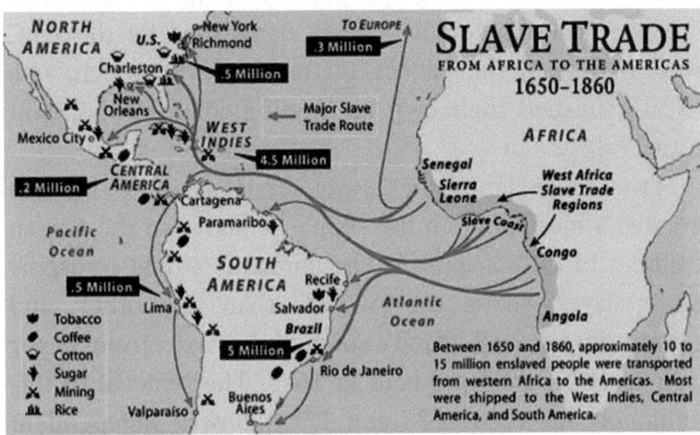

Slave Trade

CHAPTER III

Rivalry with other European empires

At the end of the 16th century, England and the Dutch Empire began to challenge the Portuguese Empire's monopoly of trade with Asia, forming private joint-stock companies to finance the voyages — the English, later British, East India Company and the Dutch East India Company, chartered in 1600 and 1602 respectively. The primary aim of these companies was to tap into the lucrative spice trade, an effort focused mainly on two regions: the East Indies archipelago, and an important hub in the trade network, India. There, they competed for trade supremacy with Portugal and with each other. Although England eclipsed the Netherlands as a colonial power, in the short term the Netherlands' more advanced financial system and the three Anglo-Dutch Wars of the 17th century left it with a stronger position in Asia. Hostilities ceased after the Glorious Revolution of 1688 when the Dutch William of Orange ascended the English throne, bringing peace between the Dutch Republic and England. A deal between the two nations left the spice trade of the East Indies archipelago to the Netherlands and the textiles industry of India to England, but textiles soon overtook spices in terms of profitability.

Peace between England and the Netherlands in 1688 meant the two countries entered the Nine Years' War as allies, but the conflict — waged in Europe and overseas between France, Spain and the Anglo-Dutch alliance — left the English a stronger colonial power than the Dutch, who were forced to devote a larger proportion of their military budget to the costly land war in Europe. The death of Charles II of Spain in 1700 and his bequeathal of Spain and its colonial empire to Philip V of Spain, a grandson of the King of France, raised the prospect of the unification of France, Spain and their respective colonies, an unacceptable state of affairs for England and the other powers of Europe. In 1701, England, Portugal and the Netherlands sided with the Holy Roman Empire against Spain and France in the War of the Spanish Succession, which lasted for thirteen years.

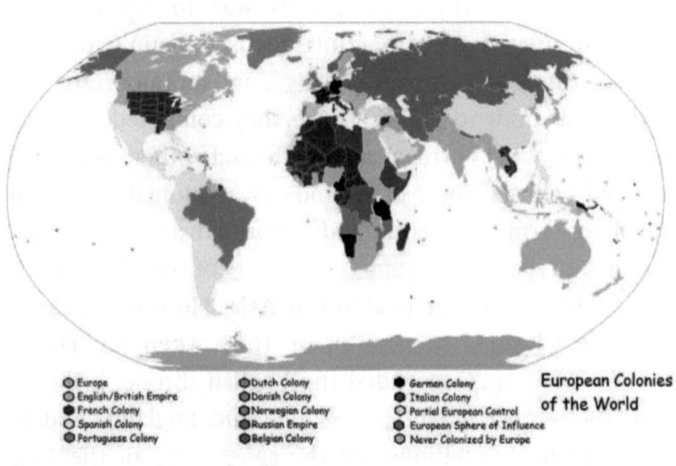

CHAPTER IV

Scottish attempt to expand overseas

In 1695, the Parliament of Scotland granted a charter to the Company of Scotland, which established a settlement in 1698 on the Isthmus of Panama. Besieged by neighbouring Spanish colonists of New Granada, and afflicted by malaria, the colony was abandoned two years later. The Darien scheme was a financial disaster for Scotland — a quarter of Scottish capital was lost in the enterprise — and ended Scottish hopes of establishing its own overseas empire. The episode had major political consequences, helping to persuade the government of the Kingdom of Scotland of the merits of turning the personal union with England into a political and economic one under the Kingdom of Great Britain established by the Acts of Union 1707.

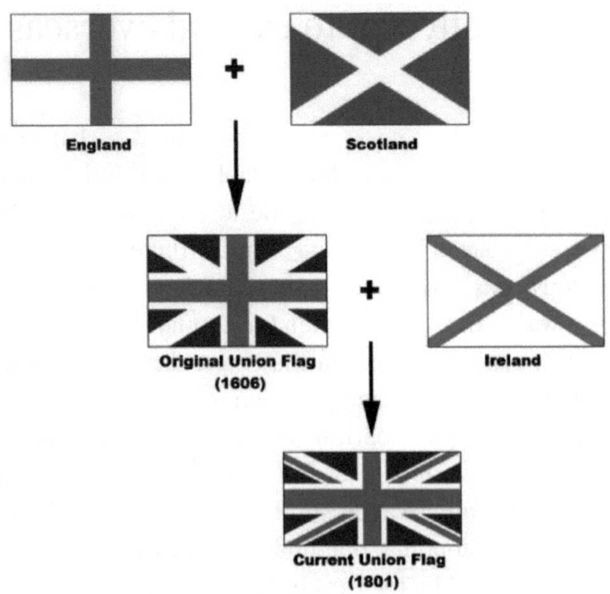
England
Scotland
Original Union Flag
(1606)
Ireland
Current Union Flag
(1801)

CHAPTER V

"First" British Empire (1707–1783)

The 18th century saw the newly united Great Britain rise to be the world's dominant colonial power, with France becoming its main rival on the imperial stage. Great Britain, Portugal, the Netherlands and the Holy Roman Empire continued the War of the Spanish Succession, which lasted until 1714 and was concluded by the Treaty of Utrecht. Philip V of Spain renounced his and his descendants' claim to the French throne, and Spain lost its empire in Europe. The British Empire was territorially enlarged: from France, Britain gained Newfoundland and Acadia, and from Spain Gibraltar and Menorca. Gibraltar became a critical naval base and allowed Britain to control the Atlantic entry and exit point to the Mediterranean. Spain ceded the rights to the lucrative asiento (permission to sell African slaves in Spanish America) to Britain. With the outbreak of the Anglo-Spanish War of Jenkins' Ear in 1739, Spanish privateers attacked British merchant shipping along the Triangle Trade routes. In 1746, the Spanish and British began peace talks, with the King of Spain agreeing to stop all attacks on British shipping; however, in the Treaty of Madrid Britain lost its slave-trading rights in Latin America.

In the East Indies, British and Dutch merchants continued to compete in spices and textiles. With textiles becoming the larger trade, by 1720, in terms of sales, the British company had overtaken the Dutch. During the middle decades of the 18th century, there were several outbreaks of military conflict on the Indian subcontinent, as the English East India Company and its French counterpart, struggled alongside local rulers to fill the vacuum that had been left by the decline of the Mughal Empire. The Battle of Plassey in 1757, in which the British defeated the Nawab of Bengal and his French allies, left the British East India Company in control of Bengal and as the major military and political power in India. France was left control of its enclaves but with military restrictions and an obligation to support British client states, ending French hopes of controlling India. In the following decades the British East India Company gradually increased the size of the territories under its control, either ruling directly or via local rulers under the threat of force from the Presidency Armies, the vast majority of which was composed of Indian sepoys, led by British officers. The British and French struggles in India became but one theatre of the global Seven Years‘ War (1756–1763) involving France, Britain, and the other major European powers.

The signing of the Treaty of Paris of 1763 had important consequences for the future of the British Empire. In North America, France's future as a colonial power effectively ended with the recognition of British claims to Rupert's Land, and the ceding of New France to Britain (leaving a sizeable French-speaking population under British control) and Louisiana to Spain. Spain ceded Florida to Britain. Along with its victory over France in India, the Seven Years' War therefore left Britain as the world's most powerful maritime power.

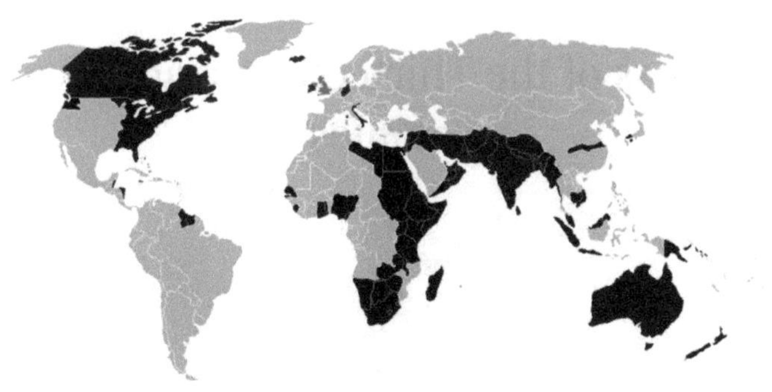

"First" British Empire (1707–1783)

CHAPTER VI

Loss of the Thirteen American Colonies

During the 1760s and early 1770s, relations between the Thirteen Colonies and Britain became increasingly strained, primarily because of resentment of the British Parliament's attempts to govern and tax American colonists without their consent. This was summarised at the time by the slogan "No taxation without representation", a perceived violation of the guaranteed Rights of Englishmen. The American Revolution began with a rejection of Parliamentary authority and moves towards self-government. In response, Britain sent troops to reimpose direct rule, leading to the outbreak of war in 1775. The following year, in 1776, the Second Continental Congress issued the Declaration of Independence proclaiming the colonies' sovereignty from the British Empire as the new United States of America. The entry of French and Spanish forces into the war tipped the military balance in the Americans' favour and after a decisive defeat at Yorktown in 1781, Britain began negotiating peace terms. American independence was acknowledged at the Peace of Paris in 1783.

The loss of such a large portion of British America, at the time Britain's most populous overseas possession, is seen by some historians as the event defining the transition between the "first" and "second" empires, in which Britain shifted its attention away from the Americas to Asia, the Pacific and later Africa. Adam Smith's Wealth of Nations, published in 1776, had argued that colonies were redundant, and that free trade should replace the old mercantilist policies that had characterised the first period of colonial expansion, dating back to the protectionism of Spain and Portugal. The growth of trade between the newly independent United States and Britain after 1783 seemed to confirm Smith's view that political control was not necessary for economic success.

The war to the south influenced British policy in Canada, where between 40,000 and 100,000 defeated Loyalists had migrated from the new United States following independence. The 14,000 Loyalists who went to the Saint John and Saint Croix river valleys, then part of Nova Scotia, felt too far removed from the provincial government in Halifax, so London split off New Brunswick as a separate colony in 1784. The Constitutional Act of 1791 created the provinces of Upper Canada (mainly English speaking) and Lower Canada (mainly French-speaking) to defuse tensions between the French and British communities and implemented governmental systems similar to those employed in Britain, with the intention of asserting imperial authority and not allowing the sort of popular control of government that was perceived to have led to the American Revolution.

Tensions between Britain and the United States escalated again during the Napoleonic Wars, as Britain tried to cut off American trade with France and boarded American ships to impress men into the Royal Navy. The United States Congress declared war, the War of 1812, and invaded Canadian territory. In response, Britain invaded the US, but the pre-war boundaries were reaffirmed by the

1814 Treaty of Ghent, ensuring Canada's future would be separate from that of the United States.

Thirteen American Colonies

CHAPTER VII

Rise of the "Second" British Empire (1783–1815)

Since 1718, transportation to the American colonies had been a penalty for various offences in Britain, with approximately one thousand convicts transported per year. Forced to find an alternative location after the loss of the Thirteen Colonies in 1783, the British government turned to Australia. The coast of Australia had been discovered for Europeans by the Dutch in 1606, but there was no attempt to colonise it. In 1770 James Cook charted the eastern coast while on a scientific voyage, claimed the continent for Britain, and named it New South Wales. In 1778, Joseph Banks, Cook's botanist on the voyage, presented evidence to the government on the suitability of Botany Bay for the establishment of a penal settlement, and in 1787 the first shipment of convicts set sail, arriving in 1788. Unusually, Australia was claimed through proclamation. Indigenous Australians were considered too uncivilised to require treaties, and colonisation brought disease and violence that together with the deliberate dispossession of land and culture were devastating to these peoples. Britain continued to transport convicts to New South Wales until 1840, to Tasmania until 1853 and to Western Australia until 1868. The Australian colonies became profitable exporters of wool and gold, mainly because of the Victorian gold rush, making its capital Melbourne for a time the richest city in the world.

During his voyage, Cook visited New Zealand, known to Europeans due to the 1642 voyage of Dutch explorer Abel Tasman, and claimed both the North and the South islands for the British crown in 1769 and 1770 respectively. Initially, interaction between the indigenous Māori population and European Pākehā settlers was limited to the trading of goods. European settlement increased through the early decades of the 19th century, with numerous trading stations established, especially in the North. In 1839, the New Zealand Company announced plans to buy large tracts of land and establish colonies in New Zealand. On 6 February 1840, Captain William Hobson and around 40 Maori chiefs signed the Treaty of Waitangi. This treaty is considered to be New Zealand's founding document, but differing interpretations of the Maori and English versions of the text have meant that it continues to be a source of dispute.

The British also expanded their mercantile interests in the North Pacific. Spain and Britain had become rivals in the area, culminating in the Nootka Crisis in 1789. Both sides mobilised for war, but when France refused to support Spain it was forced to back down, leading to the Nootka Convention. The outcome was a humiliation for Spain, which practically renounced all sovereignty on the North Pacific coast. This opened the way to British expansion in the area, and a number of expeditions took place; firstly a naval expedition led by George Vancouver which explored the inlets around the Pacific North West, particularly around Vancouver Island. On land, expeditions sought to discover a river route to the Pacific for the extension of the North American fur trade. Alexander Mackenzie of the North West Company led the first, starting out in 1792, and a year a later he became the first European to reach the Pacific overland north of the Rio Grande, reaching the ocean near present-day Bella Coola. This preceded the Lewis and Clark Expedition by twelve years. Shortly thereafter, Mackenzie's companion, John Finlay, founded the first permanent European settlement in British Columbia, Fort St. John. The North West Company sought further exploration and backed expeditions by David Thompson, starting in 1797, and later by Simon Fraser. These pushed into the wilderness territories of the Rocky Mountains and Interior Plateau to the Strait of Georgia on the Pacific Coast, expanding British North America westward.

CHAPTER VIII

Wars with France

The Battle of Waterloo in 1815 ended in the defeat of Napoleon and marked the beginning of Pax Britannica.

Britain was challenged again by France under Napoleon, in a struggle that, unlike previous wars, represented a contest of ideologies between the two nations. It was not only Britain's position on the world stage that was at risk: Napoleon threatened to invade Britain itself, just as his armies had overrun many countries of continental Europe.

The Napoleonic Wars were therefore ones in which Britain invested large amounts of capital and resources to win. French ports were blockaded by the Royal Navy, which won a decisive victory over a French Imperial Navy-Spanish Navy fleet at the Battle of Trafalgar in 1805. Overseas colonies were attacked and occupied, including those of the Netherlands, which was annexed by Napoleon in 1810. France was finally defeated by a coalition of European armies in 1815. Britain was again the beneficiary of peace treaties: France ceded the Ionian Islands, Malta (which it had occupied in 1798), Mauritius, St Lucia, the Seychelles and Tobago; Spain ceded Trinidad; the Netherlands ceded Guyana, Ceylon and the Cape Colony, while the Danish ceded Heligoland. Britain returned Guadeloupe, Martinique, French Guiana, and Réunion to France; Menorca to Spain; Danish West Indies to Denmark and Java and Suriname to the Netherlands.

CHAPTER IX

Abolition of slavery

With the advent of the Industrial Revolution, goods produced by slavery became less important to the British economy. Added to this was the cost of suppressing regular slave rebellions. With support from the British abolitionist movement, Parliament enacted the Slave Trade Act in 1807, which abolished the slave trade in the empire. In 1808, Sierra Leone Colony was designated an official British colony for freed slaves. Parliamentary reform in 1832 saw the influence of the West India Committee decline. The Slavery Abolition Act, passed the following year, abolished slavery in the British Empire on 1 August 1834, finally bringing the Empire into line with the law in the UK (with the exception of the territories administered by the East India Company and Ceylon, where slavery was ended in 1844). Under the Act, slaves were granted full emancipation after a period of four to six years of "apprenticeship". Facing further opposition from abolitionists, the apprenticeship system was abolished in 1838. The British government compensated slave-owners.

CHAPTER X

Britain's imperial century (1815–1914)

Between 1815 and 1914, a period referred to as Britain's "imperial century" by some historians, around 10 million sq mi (26 million km^2) of territory and roughly 400 million people were added to the British Empire. Victory over Napoleon left Britain without any serious international rival, other than Russia in Central Asia. Unchallenged at sea, Britain adopted the role of global policeman, a state of affairs later known as the Pax Britannica, and a foreign policy of "splendid isolation". Alongside the formal control it exerted over its own colonies, Britain's dominant position in world trade meant that it effectively controlled the economies of many countries, such as China, Argentina and Siam, which has been described by some historians as an "Informal Empire".

British imperial strength was underpinned by the steamship and the telegraph, new technologies invented in the second half of the 19th century, allowing it to control and defend the empire. By 1902, the British Empire was linked together by a network of telegraph cables, called the All Red Line.

CHAPTER XI

East India Company rule and the British Raj in India

The East India Company drove the expansion of the British Empire in Asia. The Company's army had first joined forces with the Royal Navy during the Seven Years' War, and the two continued to co-operate in arenas outside India: the eviction of the French from Egypt (1799), the capture of Java from the Netherlands (1811), the acquisition of Penang Island (1786), Singapore (1819) and Malacca (1824) and the defeat of Burma (1826).

From its base in India, the Company had been engaged in an increasingly profitable opium export trade to Qing China since the 1730s. This trade, illegal since it was outlawed by China in 1729, helped reverse the trade imbalances resulting from the British imports of tea, which saw large outflows of silver from Britain to China. In 1839, the confiscation by the Chinese authorities at Canton of 20,000 chests of opium led Britain to attack China in the First Opium War and resulted in the seizure by Britain of Hong Kong Island, at that time a minor settlement, and other Treaty Ports including Shanghai.

During the late 18th and early 19th centuries, the British Crown began to assume an increasingly large role in the affairs of the Company. A series of Acts of Parliament were passed, including the Regulating Act of 1773, Pitt's India Act of 1784 and the Charter Act of 1813 which regulated the Company's affairs and established the sovereignty of the Crown over the territories that it had acquired. The

Company's eventual end was precipitated by the Indian Rebellion in 1857, a conflict that had begun with the mutiny of sepoys, Indian troops under British officers and discipline. The rebellion took six months to suppress, with heavy loss of life on both sides. The following year the British government dissolved the Company and assumed direct control over India through the Government of India Act 1858, establishing the British Raj, where an appointed governor-general administered India and Queen Victoria was crowned the Empress of India. India became the empire's most valuable possession, "the Jewel in the Crown", and was the most important source of Britain's strength.

A series of serious crop failures in the late 19th century led to widespread famines on the subcontinent in which it is estimated that over 15 million people died. The East India Company had failed to implement any coordinated policy to deal with the famines during its period of rule. Later, under direct British rule, commissions were set up after each famine to investigate the causes and implement new policies, which took until the early 1900s to have an effect.

CHAPTER XII

Rivalry with Russia

During the 19th century, Britain and the Russian Empire vied to fill the power vacuums that had been left by the declining Ottoman Empire, Qajar dynasty and Qing dynasty. This rivalry in Central Asia came to be known as the "Great Game". As far as Britain was concerned, defeats inflicted by Russia on Persia and Turkey demonstrated its imperial ambitions and capabilities and stoked fears in Britain of an overland invasion of India. In 1839, Britain moved to pre-empt this by invading Afghanistan, but the First Anglo-Afghan War was a disaster for Britain.

When Russia invaded the Ottoman Balkans in 1853, fears of Russian dominance in the Mediterranean and the Middle East led Britain and France to enter the war in support of the Ottoman Empire and invade the Crimean Peninsula to destroy Russian naval capabilities. The ensuing Crimean War (1854–1856), which involved new techniques of modern warfare, was the only global war fought between Britain and another imperial power during the Pax Britannica and was a resounding defeat for Russia. The situation remained unresolved in Central Asia for two more decades, with Britain annexing Baluchistan in 1876 and Russia annexing Kirghizia, Kazakhstan and Turkmenistan. For a while, it appeared that another war would be inevitable, but the two countries reached an agreement on their respective spheres of influence in the region in 1878 and on all outstanding matters in 1907 with the signing of the Anglo-Russian Entente. The destruction of the Imperial Russian Navy by the Imperial Japanese

Navy at the Battle of Port Arthur during the Russo-Japanese War of 1904–1905 limited its threat to the British.

CHAPTER XIII

Cape to Cairo

The Dutch East India Company had founded the Dutch Cape Colony on the southern tip of Africa in 1652 as a way station for its ships travelling to and from its colonies in the East Indies. Britain formally acquired the colony, and its large Afrikaner (or Boer) population in 1806, having occupied it in 1795 to prevent its falling into French hands during the Flanders Campaign. British immigration to the Cape Colony began to rise after 1820, and pushed thousands of Boers, resentful of British rule, northwards to found their own—mostly short-lived—independent republics, during the Great Trek of the late 1830s and early 1840s. In the process the Voortrekkers clashed repeatedly with the British, who had their own agenda with regard to colonial expansion in South Africa and to the various native African polities, including those of the Sotho people and the Zulu Kingdom. Eventually, the Boers established two republics that had a longer lifespan: the South African Republic or Transvaal Republic (1852–1877; 1881–1902) and the Orange Free State (1854–1902). In 1902 Britain occupied both republics, concluding a treaty with the two Boer Republics following the Second Boer War (1899–1902).

In 1869 the Suez Canal opened under Napoleon III, linking the Mediterranean Sea with the Indian Ocean. Initially the Canal was opposed by the British; but once opened, its strategic value was quickly recognised and became the "jugular vein of the Empire". In 1875, the Conservative government of Benjamin Disraeli bought the indebted Egyptian ruler Isma'il Pasha's 44 per cent shareholding in the Suez Canal for £4 million (equivalent to £400 million in 2021). Although this did not grant outright control of the strategic waterway, it did give Britain leverage. Joint Anglo-French financial control over Egypt ended in outright British occupation in 1882. Although Britain controlled the Khedivate of Egypt into the 20th century, it was officially a vassal state of the Ottoman Empire and not part of the British Empire. The French were still majority shareholders and attempted to weaken the British position, but a compromise was reached with the 1888 Convention of Constantinople, which made the Canal officially neutral territory.

With competitive French, Belgian and Portuguese activity in the lower Congo River region undermining orderly colonisation of tropical Africa, the Berlin Conference of 1884–85 was held to regulate the competition between the European powers in what was called the "Scramble for Africa" by defining "effective occupation" as the criterion for international recognition of territorial claims. The scramble continued into the 1890s, and caused Britain to reconsider its decision in 1885 to withdraw from Sudan. A joint force of British and Egyptian troops defeated the Mahdist Army in 1896 and rebuffed an attempted French invasion at Fashoda in 1898. Sudan was nominally made an Anglo-Egyptian condominium, but a British colony in reality.

British gains in Southern and East Africa prompted Cecil Rhodes, pioneer of British expansion in Southern Africa, to urge a "Cape to Cairo" railway linking the strategically important Suez Canal to the mineral-rich south of the continent. During the 1880s and 1890s, Rhodes, with his privately owned British South Africa

Company, occupied and annexed territories named after him, Rhodesia.

CHAPTER XIV

Changing status of the white colonies

The path to independence for the white colonies of the British Empire began with the 1839 Durham Report, which proposed unification and self-government for Upper and Lower Canada, as a solution to political unrest which had erupted in armed rebellions in 1837. This began with the passing of the Act of Union in 1840, which created the Province of Canada. Responsible government was first granted to Nova Scotia in 1848, and was soon extended to the other British North American colonies. With the passage of the British North America Act, 1867 by the British Parliament, the Province of Canada, New Brunswick and Nova Scotia were formed into Canada, a confederation enjoying full self-government with the exception of international relations. Australia and New Zealand achieved similar levels of self-government after 1900, with the Australian colonies federating in 1901. The term "dominion status" was officially introduced at the 1907 Imperial Conference.

The last decades of the 19th century saw concerted political campaigns for Irish home rule. Ireland had been united with Britain into the United Kingdom of Great Britain and Ireland with the Act of Union 1800 after the Irish Rebellion of 1798, and had suffered a severe famine between 1845 and 1852. Home rule was supported by the British Prime minister, William Gladstone, who hoped that Ireland might follow in Canada's footsteps as a Dominion within the empire, but his 1886 Home Rule bill was defeated in Parliament. Although the bill, if passed, would have granted Ireland less autonomy within the UK than the Canadian provinces had within their own federation, many MPs feared that a partially independent Ireland might pose a security threat to Great Britain or mark the beginning of the break-up of the empire. A second Home Rule bill was defeated for similar reasons. A third bill was passed by Parliament in 1914, but not implemented because of the outbreak of the First World War leading to the 1916 Easter Rising.

CHAPTER XV

First World War

World War 1 was started in July 1914 and officially ended on November 11, 1918. Conflicts emerged among the most powerful forces in the modern world with the Austro-Hungarian Empire, Germany and the Ottoman Empire (and briefly Italy) on one side, and Britain, France, Russia, and later the United States on the other side during the war.

The war took the lives of some 20 million people and the world's great empires fell. Czarist Russia turned into reinstated as the communist Soviet Union. Imperial Germany turned into reinstated as the Weimar Republic and lost some parts of its territory in the East and West.

World War 1 started with a European conflict and gradually it developed into a World War. Militarism, nationalism, imperialism, and alliances increased the tensions among the European countries. The first reason, militarism, is known as the trend toward developing military resources, both for national defense and the protection of colonial interests.

Militarism indicated a rise in military disbursement and it extended to military and naval forces. It put more impact on the military men upon the policies of the civilian government. As a solution to problems militarism had a preference for force. This was one of the main reasons for the First World War. The second reason is there were too many alliances that frequently clashed with each other. Every country was pawning to safeguard others, creating intertwining mutual protection schemes.

They made alliances in secret, and they created a lot of mistrust and intuition among the European powers. Their general intuition stopped their diplomats to find a proper solution to many of the crises leading to war. Imperialism was the third reason for the First World War. As some areas of the world were left to colonize, nations were competing for subsisting colonies, and they were looking for enlarging their borders with adjacent countries. The fourth cause was nationalism. Nationalism is frequently insinuated to as identification with one's own country and support for the country. Nationalism contains a strong recognition of a group of personnel with a political entity.

The support of individuals for their own country can become of one's nation can become hatred of other nations. These were just some of the basic reasons for the war. Many people think that the instant reason for the war was because of the assassination of Archduke Francis Ferdinand, the successor to Austria-Hungary's throne. Archduke Ferdinand was fired and murdered due to what was thought to be a political conspiracy. The Austro-Hungarian Empire suddenly doubted Serbian conspiracy in the assassination and looked to frame a response that would both punish Serbia, and make the world respect Austria-Hungary's prestige and determination.

The Great War lasted four years. The war was finally over after four years and it took the lives of many people. On the eleventh hour of the eleventh day of the eleventh month of 1918, a cease-fire went into effect for all fighters. Though the war has been finished, the effects, are still seen perceptible in the world today.

In the aftermath of World War 1, the political, cultural, and social order of the world was drastically changed in many places, even outside the areas directly involved in the war. Old nations were removed, new nations were formed, international organizations set up, and many new and old ideas took a stronghold in people's minds.

As Europe fell in debt from war investment, inflation beset the continent. In addition to this, the buoyancy of previous decades was relinquished and a discouraging, gloomy outlook on life was adopted after people had experienced the ferocity of warfare and the effects of the war were brutal.

The War took the lives of approximately 20 million people and put a break in the economic development of several nations. The war happened between two parties consisting of more than one hundred nations. Though all of them did not send armed forces to the battlefield, they were a hoard of commodities and human resources and provided moral support to their companions. It continued for 4 long years from 1914 to 1918. Indian soldiers also took part in World War 1 as a colony of Britain from Africa and West Asia.

India had an aspiration that they might win independence. World War 1 war laid down the economy of the world. It led to food shortage, an outbreak of a pandemic, scarcity of vital items, etc. At the end of 1918, the war came to an end. The Allied Powers won the war. Both parties signed the Peace Treaty called an armistice.

Between 1914 and 1918, the lives of millions of women in Britain were overturned by the first world war. Its impact reached into every aspect of existence, from the dramatic to the humdrum.

Former domestic servants became window cleaners, gas fitters and crane drivers. They moved into the munitions factories, where their faces turned yellow and their hair green from the chemicals. They braved explosions and poisonous substances to serve their country – and to earn higher pay.

Well over 100,000 volunteered for the Women's Land Army, ruffling the gender norms of rural Britain. Others enlisted in the Women's Royal Naval Service, the Women's Army Auxiliary Corps or the Women's Royal Air Force as mechanics and drivers, cleaning, working in canteens or doing clerical work.

As wartime food shortages, rising prices and rents brought distress to poor families, the government marched into the kitchen with advice on bean fritters and barley rissoles. Manufacturers came up with a technological fix for middle-class housewives, tussling with "the servant problem". In an advertisement in the *Times* in 1917, the Suction Cleaner Company said: "Electric Housemaid: Simply connect to Electric Lamp Socket".

In 1915 the newly formed Women's Institutes were introduced to Britain from Canada. They urged women to study home economics and aimed to strengthen class harmony. A more radical approach to domestic dislocation was tried in east London. The socialist feminist, Sylvia Pankhurst, who denounced the first world war, set up a cost-price restaurant and a mother-and-baby clinic in a former pub, which she renamed The Mother's Arms. The dangers of being a baby were stressed on all political fronts, an awareness that would lead to the formation of local authority maternity and child welfare committees.

The wartime state was prepared to concede under duress. In 1915 the Glasgow Women's Housing Association took direct action to prevent the eviction of a soldier's family unable to pay the rent. Armed with peasemeal flour, women mounted angry pickets, with street after street joining the rent strike. As discontent spread beyond

Glasgow, the government introduced the Rent Restriction Act.

When women appeared doing "men's jobs", skilled men were inclined to view them as interlopers, likely to enable employers to break down craft differentials. And this was indeed what happened in some factories. But the new recruits would also assert themselves in the workplace. In July 1918, male and female munitions workers in Coventry took strike action together.

In that last year of the war, when women bus and train workers went on strike, the slogan, "Same work, same money" appeared.

Although rape was not usually systematic, it occurred frequently on all fronts during the First World War, during both invasion and occupation periods. It was often used in propaganda to discredit the other side for its barbarity and lawlessness, and this violence against women left a strong mark in people's minds at the time.

At the end of the 19th century, rape, commonly seen as an unfortunate but inevitable consequence of armed conflict, was not counted as one of the acts prohibited by the laws of war. Rape was only indirectly mentioned by the Hague Conventions of 1899 and 1907 that required occupying armies to respect "family honor and rights, the lives of persons, and private property" (Article 46). Still, the various commissions the belligerent parties set up during the First World War to investigate their enemies' crimes, all made a point of stressing the number of rapes committed in the territories invaded. These inquiry reports, often published immediately in order to discredit the other side, are the main source for historical research on this subject. Since this documentation asserted, as in the case of the French commission set up in September 1914, that: "attacks on women and girls were of unprecedented violence", and recorded acts that were mostly carried out during the early months of the war, it gave credence to the idea that a threshold of sexual violence was crossed during the First World War, particularly during periods of invasion. However, while the rape of the other side's women appears to have been neither an isolated nor an exceptional phenomenon, there is no evidence that it occurred on a massive or systematic scale. The frequent tendency in the literature to treat rape as a type of violence mainly connected with the specific period of invasion is due to an availability bias that is corrected to some extent by research into documents other than those produced by the commissions of inquiry. This additional documentation reveals information about rapes committed during occupation and military withdrawal.

When, in August 1914, the German army entered Belgium and France, its soldiers committed a large number of rapes along with other assaults on civilians. The actual number, impossible to estimate in the current state of research, was without a doubt considerably higher than the small number that was officially recorded. This is because many victims were too ashamed to report that they had been raped, and because press coverage and official discourse implied a lower number of rapes than were actually occurring. Inquiry reports into German atrocities, newspaper articles, drawings, engravings and novels gave unprecedented visibility to this wartime violence against women. The topic of German rape became a focus of representations of warfare and the enemy until the end of the war. This became a key lever in anti-German propaganda, extensively used in, for example, the Bryce Report, published in the British press in spring 1915. This report was translated into several languages and widely circulated.

In newspapers and government propaganda, the rape of women was presented as a symbol of the cowardly, criminal aggression the motherland had suffered, and it was used as a powerful tool for mobilising men to fight a just war of civilisation against barbarity. Public opinion was particularly shocked by collective rapes committed in public along with other physical violence including murder. The perpetrators appeared to be driven by a desire to humiliate female victims first, over whose bodies they asserted their domination, representing an extension of their control of territory. The humiliation of men was secondary and represented their inability to defend the women who were being put on public display. However, most of the aggressive acts appear to have been committed by single soldiers or groups of two or three, using the threat of a weapon and preferring to act with no witnesses present.

The most well researched and documented incidents of rape occurred in France and Belgium in 1914-1915, but invaders committed rape in other places and times during the war. On the Eastern Front, Russia and the Central Powers accused each other of offences against the civilian population. Cases of rape were reported by German refugees from East Prussia after the Russian invasion in 1914. In Galicia and Bukovina, the Jewish population was particularly targeted by the brutality of the Cossacks, whose pillage, destruction, murder and rape were condemned in Austro-Hungarian reports. German violence was also reported in Poland, when the Tsar had to relinquish after the Central Powers' offensive in summer 1915. However, civilians were treated much worse by the scorched-earth policy of the retreating Russian troops than by the German invaders. The documentary evidence is greater and better researched for rapes by German and Austro-Hungarian troops in Friuli and Veneto in 1917-1918 after the Italian defeat at Caporetto. These rapes were committed in a similar fashion to those in France and Belgium at the start of the war.

Most historians agree that the rapes committed by soldiers in the First World War were neither planned nor encouraged by commanding officers but merely tolerated as the undesirable but inevitable effect of a temporary slackening of military discipline. The Serbian case, however, appears to be an exception to this general pattern. Recent studies have shown that the Bulgarian occupation of southern Serbia from 1915 to 1918 gave rise to ethnic violence, including mass rapes encouraged by officers, with the aim of eliminating the Serbian and Greek populations of Macedonia. Unlike the German atrocities, these systematic aggressions committed in Serbia aroused very little reaction abroad and were not referred to in Allied propaganda.

In France, and to a lesser extent Italy, the revelation of German rapes gave rise to a controversy around the children to be born as a result. In early 1915, some sections of public opinion, believing that the "enemy's children", by their Germanic extraction, might represent a mortal danger of degeneracy for the "French race", pressed for their abortion, and even excused infanticide. The publicity these ideas received in a press vying to compete for patriotism and feed its readers' fantasies, should not be taken at face value: the supporters of eradicating German genes were only a tiny minority among politicians and senior medical figures, and the government quickly put an end to the matter by reasserting the illegality of abortion and organising the care of these children by the Assistance Publique (AP) in Paris.

From 1915 to 1921, 361 children born of German rape were taken in by the assisted children service of the Seine département and registered under the ad hoc category of "Special decisions". From this figure it has been estimated that a total number of between 1,000 and 5,000 children were born to French women raped by German soldiers during the First World War. The personal files of these children taken in by the AP in Paris, 80 percent of whom were born following aggressions committed after the first quarter of 1915, show that historiographers have too often seen rape as a violence connected with the German invasion, and have underestimated the extent of sexual aggression committed after the frontline had stabilised.

The occupation period saw rape where the perpetrator, usually acting alone, knew his victim, at least by sight, and did not always abscond after his crime. The requisition of military billets and female labour in fields and factories created situations particularly likely to lead to aggression, which often occurred after a period of days or months of non-violent acquaintance. To subdue their victims, the soldier rapists used blows and the threat of a weapon, but the violence could also be more emotional than physical, and would increase over time in some instances. Some women described the hunger that they and their children were forced to endure by soldiers who, before the women gave in, would offer them food for sex; in other cases, the climate of fear and a sense of powerlessness among the residents of the occupied territories was enough for a soldier to obtain a victim's submission.

Although these occupation-period rapes are beginning to be better understood, other aspects of the subject remain understudied. Research into the Eastern Front is largely lacking. Similarly, little work has been done on the aggressions committed by the winning side, for example, after the autumn of 1918, the rape of German women was increasingly alluded to in the correspondence of French soldiers who were about to occupy the Rhineland. Despite a few cases recorded by historians, particularly of sexual aggression by British soldiers in France, rape within populations not at war is also a subject that is poorly researched.

Whereas rape by the enemy loomed large in the minds of the peoples involved in the war and was a recurring theme in some national propaganda, no mention was made of it in post-war commemorations and discussions. Although explicitly added to the number of war crimes at the Peace Conference that opened in Paris in January 1919, rape quickly disappeared from the talks. It was not until 1949, following the Second World War, when sexual violence had occurred on a far greater scale than in the First World War, that rape was specifically prohibited by the laws of war.

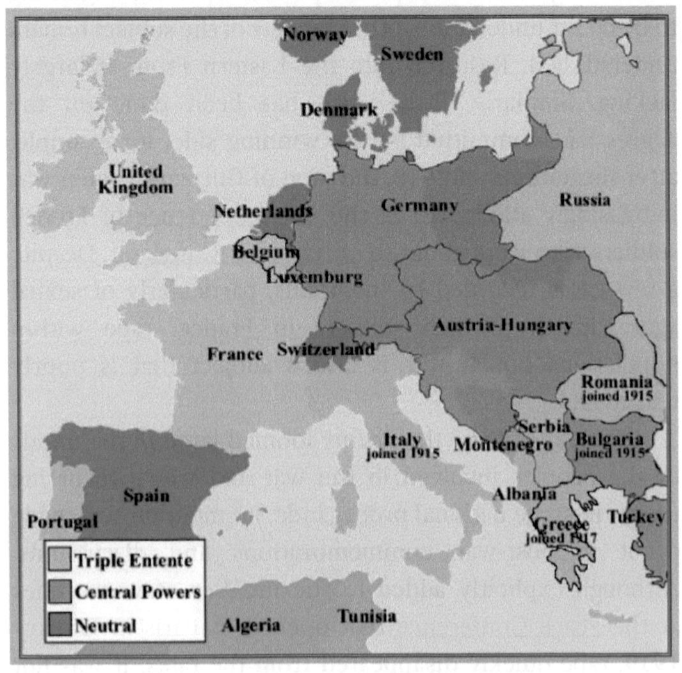

Europe in 1914

CHAPTER XVI

Inter-war period

The changing world order that the war had brought about, in particular the growth of the United States and Japan as naval powers and the rise of independence movements in India and Ireland, caused a major reassessment of British imperial policy. Forced to choose between alignment with the United States or Japan, Britain opted not to renew its Anglo-Japanese Alliance and instead signed the 1922 Washington Naval Treaty, where Britain accepted naval parity with the United States. This decision was the source of much debate in Britain during the 1930s as militaristic governments took hold in Germany and Japan helped in part by the Great Depression, for it was feared that the empire could not survive a simultaneous attack by both nations. The issue of the empire's security was a serious concern in Britain, as it was vital to the British economy.

In 1919, the frustrations caused by delays to Irish home rule led the MPs of Sinn Féin, a pro-independence party that had won a majority of the Irish seats in the 1918 British general election, to establish an independent parliament in Dublin, at which Irish independence was declared. The Irish Republican Army simultaneously began a guerrilla war against the British administration. The Irish War of Independence ended in 1921 with a stalemate and the signing of the Anglo-Irish Treaty, creating the Irish Free State, a Dominion within the British Empire, with effective internal independence but still constitutionally linked with the British Crown. Northern Ireland, consisting of six of the 32 Irish counties which had been established as a devolved region under the 1920 Government of Ireland Act, immediately exercised its option under the treaty to retain its existing status within the United Kingdom.

A similar struggle began in India when the Government of India Act 1919 failed to satisfy the demand for independence. Concerns over communist and foreign plots following the Ghadar conspiracy ensured that war-time strictures were renewed by the Rowlatt Acts. This led to tension, particularly in the Punjab region, where repressive measures culminated in the Amritsar Massacre. In Britain, public opinion was divided over the morality of the massacre, between those who saw it as having saved India from anarchy, and those who viewed it with revulsion. The non-cooperation movement was called off in March 1922 following the Chauri Chaura incident, and discontent continued to simmer for the next 25 years.

In 1922, Egypt, which had been declared a British protectorate at the outbreak of the First World War, was granted formal independence, though it continued to be a British client state until 1954. British troops remained stationed in Egypt until the signing of the Anglo-Egyptian Treaty in 1936, under which it was agreed that the troops would withdraw but continue to occupy and defend the Suez Canal zone. In return, Egypt was assisted in joining the League of Nations. Iraq, a British mandate since 1920, gained membership of the League in its own right after achieving independence from Britain in 1932. In Palestine, Britain was presented with the problem of mediating between the Arabs and increasing numbers of Jews. The Balfour Declaration, which had been incorporated into the terms of the mandate, stated that a national home for the Jewish people would be established in Palestine, and Jewish immigration allowed up to a limit that would be determined by the mandatory power. This led to increasing conflict with the Arab population, who openly revolted in 1936. As the threat of war with Germany increased during the 1930s, Britain judged the support of Arabs as more important than the establishment of a Jewish homeland, and shifted to a pro-Arab stance, limiting Jewish immigration and in turn triggering a Jewish insurgency.

The right of the Dominions to set their own foreign policy, independent of Britain, was recognised at the 1923 Imperial Conference. Britain's request for military assistance from the Dominions at the outbreak of the Chanak Crisis the previous year had been turned down by Canada and South Africa, and Canada had refused to be bound by the 1923 Treaty of Lausanne. After pressure from the Irish Free State and South Africa, the 1926 Imperial Conference issued the Balfour Declaration of 1926, declaring the Dominions to be "autonomous Communities within the British Empire, equal in status, in no way subordinate one to another" within a "British Commonwealth of Nations". This declaration was given legal substance under the 1931 Statute of Westminster. The parliaments of Canada, Australia, New Zealand, the Union of South Africa, the Irish Free State and Newfoundland were now independent of British legislative control, they could nullify British laws and Britain could no longer pass laws for them without their consent. Newfoundland reverted to colonial status in 1933, suffering from financial difficulties during the Great Depression. In 1937 the Irish Free State introduced a republican constitution renaming itself Ireland.

Europe in Interwar Period

CHAPTER XVII

Second World War

World War 2 or the Second World War is the most extensive known global human warfare to date that lasted from the year 1939 to 1945. The war was waged between two opposing military alliances: Allies and Axis, involving the majority of the Global powers and many participating countries from across Europe and the world.

It was the first state of total war where every economic, scientific and industrial resource and labour of the participating countries were dedicated to waging full-scale warfare, eliminating military and civilian resources. The war involved over 100 million military personnel from more than 30 countries resulting in 70 to 85 million fatal casualties.

The history of this world is incomplete without the inclusion of the Second World War or World War 2, the most vicious and gruelling warfare waged by humans against each other. It involved the vast majority of the countries and Global powers during the period 1939 to 1945.

The war was primarily waged between two opposing military alliances: The Allies mainly comprising the United Kingdom & British Empire, the Third Republic of France, Soviet Union, United States of America and their allies, and the Axis Powers involving Nazi Germany, Fascist Italy, Empire of Japan and their allies.

It started on 1st September 1939, when Nazi Germany invaded Poland and placid support from the Soviet Union and the subsequent declaration of war on Germany by

Poland's allies, France and the United Kingdom. Germany's Axis Powers had significant gains in the earlier years of the Second World war, mainly between 1939 to 1941 when it conquered and dominated much of continental Europe and parts of Africa.

The largest gain on the Axis side came with the rapid defeat of France at the hands of Germany due to Germany's advanced warfare technique of Blitzkrieg that involved multi-frontier attack using infantry and armoured divisions. Adolf Hitler, the Dictator/ Fuhrer of Germany during the war, is mainly attributed as the perpetrator of the war due to his Nationalist Fascist and Racial supremacy-based political ideology leading to Germany's aggressive stance in much of continental Europe.

With France's fall in 1940, the war was primarily waged between the Axis Powers and the British Empire, with minor gains and losses on both sides. It was a multi-frontier conflict with battles occurring in various regions, including mainland Europe, Eurasia, the Balkans, the Atlantic, and the Pacific Ocean, East Asia, and Northern and Central Africa, and Ariel attacks on the British Isles.

FRANCE OCCUPIED BY AXIS POWERS
1940-1944

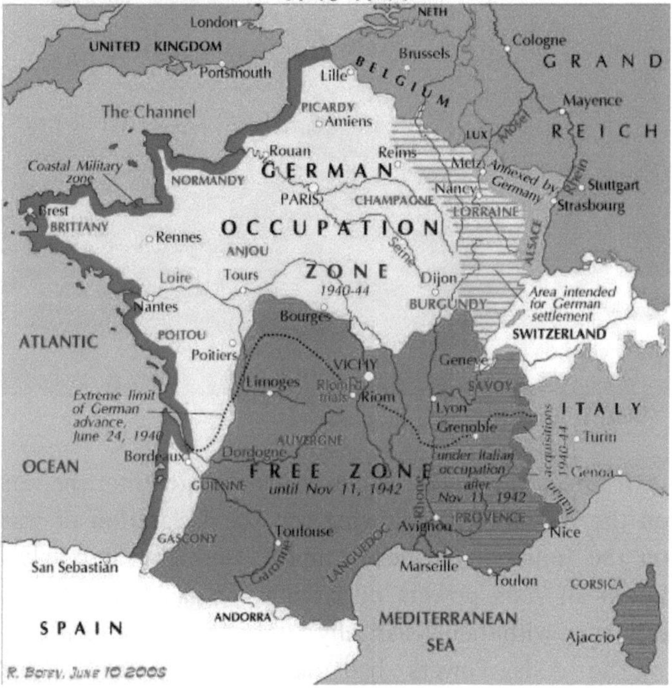

The war took a significant turn in 1941 with two significant events:

1. The Invasion of Soviet Russia and its Union in June 1941
2. Leading to the largest land warfare in human history
3. The Pearl Harbour bombing by Japanese Kamikaze in December 1941

It forced the United States of America to enter the war on the Allies side. Following the US declaration of war on the Imperial Japanese Empire, Germany and Italy's European Axis powers declared war against the US in solidarity with their Asian Ally.

The Axis Powers had significant strategic gains throughout 1941, including Imperial Japan. It captured and dominated much of the Western Pacific, Eastern China and Manchuria, and Southern Asia. However, its advances were obstructed after a significant naval defeat at the US navy's hands at the Battle of Midway on the Pacific Ocean. Fascist Italy subsequently suffered significant defeats in North Africa and the Balkans and eventually surrendered to the Allies with their Fascist Dictator, Benito Mussolini, being publicly executed.

The collective Allied invasions of Sicily and the Italian Mainland in 1943, along with German defeat at the Eastern front, forced the Axis powers to retreat on all fronts strategically. The war was concluded in 1945 with the Allied invasion of German-controlled territories, the fall of Berlin at the Soviet Union's hands, and the Nuclear Bombing of Hiroshima and Nagasaki in Japan by the United States of America.

World War 2 was the largest war ever waged in human history lasting from 1939 to 1945 between two primary military alliances, the Allies and the Axis. It started with Poland's invasion by Nazi Germany and Communist Soviet Union after the secret Molotov-Ribbentrop pact between the two powers that led France and the United Kingdom to declare war on Germany.

The war occurred on multiple battlefronts and involved more than 100 million soldiers from over 30 countries from across the globe. It resulted in a collective casualty of over 80 million military as well as civilian deaths.

It ended with the Axis defeat after the fall of Berlin and the Nuclear Bombing of the Japanese cities of Hiroshima and Nagasaki by the United States. It had a profound effect on the subsequent world politics and histories like the eventual fall of the British and French Empires and their colonies' independence, significant shifts in global politics, and the United Nations' formation.

The historical record of sexual violence at the wartime, especially World War II is silent to preserve masculine honour and female purity as scholars argued. The voices of victims and atrocities of sexual violence did not get a considerable amount of care. Moreover, the historical attempts have highly focussed on the condemnation of masculine, feminine and community honour caused by sexual violence. The mentioned referring to shaming and embarrassing the male counterparts for their incapability to protect the 'honour' of 'their' women. The other factors for the secrecy of sexual violence are social and cultural discomfort with sex and sexual violence wherein victims feel ashamed and stigmatised to recount their sexual victimization. Besides, scholars have witnessed that somewhat misogyny of historians and policymakers who didn't feel essential to take into account of the women experiences of violence.

The **'comfort women' of the Imperial Japanese Army** in WW II is the most extreme institutionalised sexual violence against women. The scholars have argued that euphemism 'comfort women' that masked the gravity of government-sponsored human trafficking. The motivation for creating 'comfort women and station' was not to repeat the history of mass rape that Japanese soldier did in Nanking, China that could have demolished the public image of Japan. With the fear of the country's reputation in the eye of the world, the Japanese emperor initiated the system of 'comfort women' also a reward to soldiers fighting for the Japanese Empire. The other justifications provided by Japanese Army for implementation and maintaining of Comfort women station to prevent rape by the former that could raise the hostility of inhabitants of the occupied area; to boost the army morale; to discipline the behaviour of soldiers. Despite, of Rules of Use for Military Comfort station, created by the Japanese military to avoid abuse on comfort women, none of the soldiers abided it and thousands of women got victimized. Comfort women involved unmarried young women as young as twelve years old primarily from Korea and China and other Southeast Asian countries who Japanese deemed as culturally inferior people. These comfort women got either enticed with the false promise of receiving jobs such as housework or they got kidnapped/coercively recruited. Eventually, they ended up in the brothels/camp stations nearby the war zones wherein they got forced to serve 30-40 soldiers per day without any rest and pay. According to the testimony of Yong Soo Lee, the comfort women survivor, she commented that *"it was not a comfort station, it was slaughterhouse"* wherein the women were beaten, tortured or killed if they refuse to provide *'comfort'* to the Japanese soldier. If these *'comfort women'* got sick they got killed, there was no medical assistance provided to them. Besides, the comfort camps were mostly situated in foreign lands, hence their mobility got constrained because even if they tried to escape they had no place to go because of the language barrier or if they got caught for getting escaped they were publicly tortured and killed. The comfort women weren't even buried after their death, they were just left stranded. Reiterating, this all occurred under the supervision of Japan government official who even established rules and regulations for this system but it turned blind eye inside the system. After the war ended, many of the comfort women got killed in military actions or they were left abandoned. Some who found their way home got shunned by their community, labelled as 'dirty' and socially and culturally stigmatised thereby not allowed to speak about their experiences.

Proceeding to **Nazi camp brothel**, the image one can have is Jewish women exploited for the sexual gratification of Nazis soldiers. However, the reality is contrary to the mentioned. In the final year of the Nazi concentration camp, brothels were installed for the prisoners. It was the brainchild of Heinrich Himmler, chief of the economic and administrative main office of the SS, who wanted to extract the productivity of camp prisoners for Furher's megalomaniacal construction projects and these projects needed building materials to fulfil Hitler's plan of redesigning the major German cities such as Berlin, Weimar, Munich, Linz and Hamburg. Himmler ideated that establishment of brothels as the sexual incentive for the hard-working prisoners to increase their efficiency of production but at the expense of forced sex slavery of women. The Russians and Jews prisoners were exempted from approaching the sex workers. These brothel camps got built in a quiet bureaucratic manner wherein strict Nazis race rules were followed. In other words, the German prisoner can only go to German women. Furthermore, the purpose Himmler had for these brothels and forced sexual slavery was also to keep homosexuality at bay since there was a fear of breaking out among the prisoners. About 300-400 women, especially from the camp of Ravensbruk and Auschwitz, were forced into prostitution in ten concentration camps and the territories occupied by the Nazi. The women selected for forced prostitution were young women who had either displayed anti-social behaviour or suspected of having political ties or relationships with Jews. These women were in Auschwitz and Ravensburk camp who were construction worker. A false promise was made to them of release from the camps after six months of work in the brothel. These women had no option between life and death. For instance, according to polish prisoner women working as construction worker she *'volunteered'* for the brothel because she could not survive winter in Auschwitz as a field worker and preferred forced sex labourer. For some women, it was desperation to get one more slice of bread and soup. According to the testimony of one of the prisoners from Ravensburk who got *'voluntarily'* tempted into forced prostitution, maintains that *"They told us we were in the camp brothel, that we were the lucky ones. We would eat well and have enough to drink. If we behaved and fulfilled our duties nothing would happen to us"*. These women had to have sex with average 8-10 men every night between 8 PM-10 PM not allowed giving more than 15 mins to each prisoner. It was made sure by SS prisoner who used to guard it through the elaborate system of *'spy holes'*. The women were humiliated by frequent medical checkups and disinfected creams coated over their genitals before and after the act more like treated them as machines of sexual gratification. After the liberation from the camp, these women got shunned to share their experience out of shame or trauma while foreign victims feared that might be perceived as collaborators with Nazis campaign. Until 2002, they didn't get the recognition of from the German government as a victim of sex slavery or any compensation for their ordeal.

Lastly, as WW II was fading away, the victorious Soviet Soldiers or the Red Army racing towards Berlin in 1945 raped one and half a million German women. Through the **rape of 'German Women'**, they wanted to show the defeat of Nazi Germany. There were notorious mass rapes and multiple rapes on a single woman from April 24 to May 5, 1945, when Soviets secured Berlin. They were raping every German woman ageing from eight to eighty. A diary of a woman journalist was retrieved – *"A woman in Berlin: Eight weeks in the conquered city"* – who provided the detailed account on the ways German women got raped and the choices the latter had to make for survival. Besides, the Soviet army raped the Jewish women who already went into the torment in the Nazi concentration camp. The journalist provided the detailed account on how one of the Jewish couples who were hiding from Nazi for months in a basement came out when they saw Red Army as their liberators but the husband was fatally shot while his wife was *"[taken] into the hallway, three men on top of her, as she kept howling and screaming, "But I'm Jewish, I'm Jewish"*. The journalist describes that for survival the German women entered into an informal agreement with Soviet Soldiers and officers called as 'Ivans' from the protection from the other Red Armies. While some women opted for prostitution to stay alive and to avoid multiple rapes by being consort to a soviet soldier. The line between prostitution and rape got blurred by the end of WW II.

According to scholars narrative, the German women were getting punished for the crimes done by German men in USSR as a form of justice. The rapes were done with the motive of devaluation and humiliation of German woman also to challenge the masculinity of German men and direct attack to the German corporate body. Red Army did not distinguish between ethnicity and class when it came to rape. But more astounding was German man reactions to the raped women. Eventually, victims of rape were blamed for their irrepressibility for the Soviet soldiers. Through the above case studies deliberation, an observation is made that sexual violence becomes a weapon of war at the wartime period when it involves strategic campaigns. In other words, there are pre-determined political or military or economic objectives to be achieved. The weapon of war is defined as *'instrument of terror'* to control, coerce or erasure of targetted populations. Conventionally, the understanding of sexual violence during the period of war is limited to rape (kate). Notwithstanding, the case studies here addressed that there are other forms of sexual violence used in war-conflict situations that vary in intensity and ultimately take its distinct appearance. These are sexual slavery, trafficking, undressing, sexual mutilation, forced marriage, branding are commonly used violence during the wartime period. The sexual atrocities inflicted upon the women at the time of World War II vary in the conduct depended upon countries disposition in war during world war II complementing with their strategic campaigns wherein the sexual gratification of the perpetrators was in common. These case studies reflected that imperialist and axis countries along with the allies, called good guys fighting for the good wars and cause, had equally participated in the barbarous act of sexual violence.

CHAPTER XVIII

Decolonisation and decline

Though Britain and the empire emerged victorious from the Second World War, the effects of the conflict were profound, both at home and abroad. Much of Europe, a continent that had dominated the world for several centuries, was in ruins, and host to the armies of the United States and the Soviet Union, who now held the balance of global power. Britain was left essentially bankrupt, with insolvency only averted in 1946 after the negotiation of a US$ 4.33 billion loan from the United States, the last installment of which was repaid in 2006. At the same time, anti-colonial movements were on the rise in the colonies of European nations. The situation was complicated further by the increasing Cold War rivalry of the United States and the Soviet Union. In principle, both nations were opposed to European colonialism. In practice, American anti-communism prevailed over anti-imperialism, and therefore the United States supported the continued existence of the British Empire to keep Communist expansion in check. At first British politicians believed it would be possible to maintain Britain's role as a world power at the head of a re-imagined Commonwealth, but by 1960 they were forced to recognise that there was an irresistible "wind of change" blowing. Their priorities changed to maintaining an extensive zone of British influence and ensuring that stable, non-Communist governments were established in former colonies. In this context, while other European powers such as France and Portugal waged costly and unsuccessful wars to keep their empires intact, Britain generally adopted a policy of peaceful disengagement from its colonies. In reality, this was rarely peaceable or altruistic. Between 1945 and 1965, the number of people under British rule outside the UK itself fell from 700 million to 5 million, 3 million of whom were in Hong Kong.

CHAPTER XIX

Initial disengagement

The pro-decolonisation Labour government, elected at the 1945 general election and led by Clement Attlee, moved quickly to tackle the most pressing issue facing the empire: Indian independence. India's two major political parties — the Indian National Congress (led by Mahatma Gandhi) and the Muslim League (led by Muhammad Ali Jinnah) — had been campaigning for independence for decades, but disagreed as to how it should be implemented. Congress favoured a unified secular Indian state, whereas the League, fearing domination by the Hindu majority, desired a separate Islamic state for Muslim-majority regions. Increasing civil unrest and the mutiny of the Royal Indian Navy during 1946 led Attlee to promise independence no later than 30 June 1948. When the urgency of the situation and risk of civil war became apparent, the newly appointed (and last) Viceroy, Lord Mountbatten, hastily brought forward the date to 15 August 1947. The borders drawn by the British to broadly partition India into Hindu and Muslim areas left tens of millions as minorities in the newly independent states of India and Pakistan. Millions of Muslims crossed from India to Pakistan and Hindus vice versa, and violence between the two communities cost hundreds of thousands of lives. Burma, which had been administered as part of the British Raj, and Sri Lanka gained their independence the following year in 1948. India, Pakistan and Sri Lanka became members of the Commonwealth, while Burma chose not to join.

The British Mandate in Palestine, where an Arab majority lived alongside a Jewish minority, presented the British with a similar problem to that of India. The matter was complicated by large numbers of Jewish refugees seeking to be admitted to Palestine following the Holocaust, while Arabs were opposed to the creation of a Jewish state. Frustrated by the intractability of the problem, attacks by Jewish paramilitary organisations and the increasing cost of maintaining its military presence, Britain announced in 1947 that it would withdraw in 1948 and leave the matter to the United Nations to solve. The UN General Assembly subsequently voted for a plan to partition Palestine into a Jewish and an Arab state. It was immediately followed by the outbreak of a civil war between the Arabs and Jews of Palestine, and British forces withdrew amid the fighting. The British Mandate for Palestine officially terminated at midnight on 15 May 1948 as the State of Israel declared independence and the 1948 Arab-Israeli War broke out, during which the territory of the former Mandate was partitioned between Israel and the surrounding Arab states. Amid the fighting, British forces continued to withdraw from Israel, with the last British troops departing from Haifa on 30 June 1948.

Following the surrender of Japan in the Second World War, anti-Japanese resistance movements in Malaya turned their attention towards the British, who had moved to quickly retake control of the colony, valuing it as a source of rubber and tin. The fact that the guerrillas were primarily Malaysian Chinese Communists meant that the British attempt to quell the uprising was supported by the Muslim Malay majority, on the understanding that once the insurgency had been quelled, independence would be granted. The Malayan Emergency, as it was called, began in 1948 and lasted until 1960, but by 1957, Britain felt confident enough to grant independence to the Federation of Malaya within the Commonwealth. In 1963, the 11 states of the federation together with Singapore, Sarawak and North Borneo joined to form Malaysia, but in 1965 Chinese-majority Singapore was expelled from the union following tensions between the Malay and Chinese populations and became an independent city-state. Brunei, which had been a British protectorate since 1888, declined to join the union.

CHAPTER XX

Suez Crisis

In the 1951 general election, the Conservative Party returned to power in Britain under the leadership of Winston Churchill. Churchill and the Conservatives believed that Britain's position as a world power relied on the continued existence of the empire, with the base at the Suez Canal allowing Britain to maintain its pre-eminent position in the Middle East in spite of the loss of India. Churchill could not ignore Gamal Abdul Nasser's new revolutionary government of Egypt that had taken power in 1952, and the following year it was agreed that British troops would withdraw from the Suez Canal zone and that Sudan would be granted self-determination by 1955, with independence to follow. Sudan was granted independence on 1 January 1956.

In July 1956, Nasser unilaterally nationalised the Suez Canal. The response of Anthony Eden, who had succeeded Churchill as Prime Minister, was to collude with France to engineer an Israeli attack on Egypt that would give Britain and France an excuse to intervene militarily and retake the canal. Eden infuriated US President Dwight D. Eisenhower by his lack of consultation, and Eisenhower refused to back the invasion. Another of Eisenhower's concerns was the possibility of a wider war with the Soviet Union after it threatened to intervene on the Egyptian side. Eisenhower applied financial leverage by threatening to sell US reserves of the British pound and thereby precipitate a collapse of the British currency. Though the invasion force was militarily successful in its objectives, UN intervention and

US pressure forced Britain into a humiliating withdrawal of its forces, and Eden resigned.

The Suez Crisis very publicly exposed Britain's limitations to the world and confirmed Britain's decline on the world stage and its end as a first-rate power, demonstrating that henceforth it could no longer act without at least the acquiescence, if not the full support, of the United States. The events at Suez wounded British national pride, leading one Member of Parliament (MP) to describe it as "Britain's Waterloo" and another to suggest that the country had become an "American satellite". Margaret Thatcher later described the mindset she believed had befallen Britain's political leaders after Suez where they "went from believing that Britain could do anything to an almost neurotic belief that Britain could do nothing", from which Britain did not recover until the successful recapture of the Falkland Islands from Argentina in 1982.

While the Suez Crisis caused British power in the Middle East to weaken, it did not collapse. Britain again deployed its armed forces to the region, intervening in Oman (1957), Jordan (1958) and Kuwait (1961), though on these occasions with American approval, as the new Prime Minister Harold Macmillan's foreign policy was to remain firmly aligned with the United States. Although Britain granted Kuwait independence in 1961, it continued to maintain a military presence in the Middle East for another decade. On 16 January 1968, a few weeks after the devaluation of the pound, Prime Minister Harold Wilson and his Defence SecretaryDenis Healey announced that British Armed Forces troops would be withdrawn from major military bases East of Suez, which included the ones in the Middle East, and primarily from Malaysia and Singapore by the end of 1971, instead of 1975 as earlier planned. By that time over 50,000 British military personnel were still stationed in the Far East, including 30,000 in Singapore. The British granted independence to the Maldives in 1965 but continued to station a garrison there until 1976, withdrew from Aden in 1967, and granted independence to Bahrain, Qatar, and the United Arab Emirates in 1971.

CHAPTER XXI

Wind of change

By the end of the 1960s in Africa, all but Rhodesia (the future Zimbabwe) and the South African mandate of South West Africa (Namibia) had achieved recognised independence.

Macmillan gave a speech in Cape Town, South Africa in February 1960 where he spoke of "the wind of change blowing through this continent". Macmillan wished to avoid the same kind of colonial war that France was fighting in Algeria, and under his premiership decolonisation proceeded rapidly. To the three colonies that had been granted independence in the 1950s — Sudan, the Gold Coast and Malaya — were added nearly ten times that number during the 1960s.

Britain's remaining colonies in Africa, except for self-governingSouthern Rhodesia, were all granted independence by 1968. British withdrawal from the southern and eastern parts of Africa was not a peaceful process. Kenyan independence was preceded by the eight-year Mau Mau uprising, in which tens of thousands of suspected rebels were interned by the colonial government in detention camps. In Rhodesia, the 1965 Unilateral Declaration of Independence by the white minority resulted in a civil war that lasted until the Lancaster House Agreement of 1979, which set the terms for recognised independence in 1980, as the new nation of Zimbabwe.

In Cyprus, a guerrilla war waged by the Greek Cypriot organisation EOKA against British rule, was ended in 1959 by the London and Zürich Agreements, which resulted in

Cyprus being granted independence in 1960. The UK retained the military bases of Akrotiri and Dhekelia as sovereign base areas. The Mediterranean colony of Malta was amicably granted independence from the UK in 1964 and became the country of Malta, though the idea had been raised in 1955 of integration with Britain.

Most of the UK's Caribbean territories achieved independence after the departure in 1961 and 1962 of Jamaica and Trinidad from the West Indies Federation, established in 1958 in an attempt to unite the British Caribbean colonies under one government, but which collapsed following the loss of its two largest members. Jamaica attained independence in 1962, as did Trinidad and Tobago. Barbados achieved independence in 1966 and the remainder of the eastern Caribbean islands, including the Bahamas, in the 1970s and 1980s, but Anguilla and the Turks and Caicos Islands opted to revert to British rule after they had already started on the path to independence. The British Virgin Islands, The Cayman Islands and Montserrat opted to retain ties with Britain, while Guyana achieved independence in 1966. Britain's last colony on the American mainland, British Honduras, became a self-governing colony in 1964 and was renamed Belize in 1973, achieving full independence in 1981. A dispute with Guatemala over claims to Belize was left unresolved.

British Overseas Territories in the Pacific acquired independence in the 1970s beginning with Fiji in 1970 and ending with Vanuatu in 1980. Vanuatu's independence was delayed because of political conflict between English and French-speaking communities, as the islands had been jointly administered as a condominium with France. Fiji, Papua New Guinea, Solomon Islands and Tuvalu became Commonwealth realms.

CHAPTER XXII

End of empire

By 1981, aside from a scattering of islands and outposts, the process of decolonisation that had begun after the Second World War was largely complete. In 1982, Britain's resolve in defending its remaining overseas territories was tested when Argentina invaded the Falkland Islands, acting on a long-standing claim that dated back to the Spanish Empire. Britain's successful military response to retake the Falkland Islands during the ensuing Falklands War contributed to reversing the downward trend in Britain's status as a world power.

The 1980s saw Canada, Australia and New Zealand sever their final constitutional links with Britain. Although granted legislative independence by the Statute of Westminster 1931, vestigial constitutional links had remained in place. The British Parliament retained the power to amend key Canadian constitutional statutes, meaning that effectively an act of the British Parliament was required to make certain changes to the Canadian Constitution. The British Parliament had the power to pass laws extending to Canada at Canadian request. Although no longer able to pass any laws that would apply as Australian Commonwealth law, the British Parliament retained the power to legislate for the individual Australian states. With regard to New Zealand, the British Parliament retained the power to pass legislation applying to New Zealand with the New Zealand Parliament's consent. In 1982, the last legal link between Canada and Britain was severed by the Canada Act 1982, which was passed by the British parliament, formally patriating the Canadian Constitution. The act ended the need for British involvement in changes to the Canadian constitution. Similarly, the Australia Act 1986 (effective 3 March 1986) severed the constitutional link between Britain and the Australian states, while New Zealand's Constitution Act 1986 (effective 1 January 1987) reformed the constitution of New Zealand to sever its constitutional link with Britain.

On 1 January 1984, Brunei, Britain's last remaining Asian protectorate, was granted independence. Independence had been delayed due to the opposition of the Sultan, who had preferred British protection.

In September 1982 the Prime Minister, Margaret Thatcher, travelled to Beijing to negotiate with the Chinese Communist government, on the future of Britain's last major and most populous overseas territory, Hong Kong. Under the terms of the 1842 Treaty of Nanking and 1860 Convention of Peking, Hong Kong Island and Kowloon Peninsula had been respectively ceded to Britain in perpetuity, but the majority of the colony consisted of the New Territories, which had been acquired under a 99-year lease in 1898, due to expire in 1997. Thatcher, seeing parallels with the Falkland Islands, initially wished to hold Hong Kong and proposed British administration with Chinese sovereignty, though this was rejected by China. A deal was reached in 1984—under the terms of the Sino-British Joint Declaration, Hong Kong would become a special administrative region of the People's Republic of China. The handover ceremony in 1997 marked for many, including Charles, Prince of Wales, who was in attendance, "the end of Empire".

CHAPTER XXIII

Legacy

Britain retains sovereignty over 14 territories outside the British Isles. In 1983, the British Nationality Act 1981 renamed the existing Crown Colonies as "British Dependent Territories", and in 2002 they were renamed the British Overseas Territories. Most former British colonies and protectorates are members of the Commonwealth of Nations, a voluntary association of equal members, comprising a population of around 2.2 billion people. Fifteen Commonwealth realms voluntarily continue to share the British monarch, Queen Elizabeth II, as their head of state. These fifteen nations are distinct and equal legal entities – the United Kingdom, Australia, Canada, New Zealand, Antigua and Barbuda, The Bahamas, Belize, Grenada, Jamaica, Papua New Guinea, Saint Kitts and Nevis, Saint Lucia, Saint Vincent and the Grenadines, Solomon Islands and Tuvalu.

Decades, and in some cases centuries, of British rule and emigration have left their mark on the independent nations that arose from the British Empire. The empire established the use of the English language in regions around the world. Today it is the primary language of up to 460 million people and is spoken by about 1.5 billion as a first, second or foreign language. Individual and team sports developed in Britain, particularly football, cricket, lawn tennis and golf were exported. British missionaries who travelled around the globe often in advance of soldiers and civil servants spread Protestantism (including Anglicanism) to all continents. The British Empire provided refuge for religiously persecuted continental Europeans for hundreds of years.

Political boundaries drawn by the British did not always reflect homogeneous ethnicities or religions, contributing to conflicts in formerly colonised areas. The British Empire was responsible for large migrations of peoples. Millions left the British Isles, with the founding settler colonist populations of the United States, Canada, Australia and New Zealand coming mainly from Britain and Ireland. Tensions remain between the white settler populations of these countries and their indigenous minorities, and between white settler minorities and indigenous majorities in South Africa and Zimbabwe. Settlers in Ireland from Great Britain have left their mark in the form of divided nationalist and unionist communities in Northern Ireland. Millions of people moved to and from British colonies, with large numbers of Overseas Indian people emigrating to other parts of the empire, such as Malaysia and Fiji, and Overseas Chinese people to Malaysia, Singapore and the Caribbean. The demographics of the United Kingdom itself were changed after the Second World War owing to immigration to Britain from its former colonies.

In the 19th century, innovation in Britain led to revolutionary changes in manufacturing, the development of factory systems, and the growth of transportation by railway and steamship. British colonial architecture, such as in churches, railway stations and government buildings, can be seen in many cities that were once part of the British Empire. The British choice of system of measurement, the imperial system, continues to be used in some countries in various ways. The convention of driving on the left-hand side of the road has been retained in much of the former empire.

The Westminster system of parliamentary democracy has served as the template for the governments for many former colonies, and English common law for legal systems. International commercial contracts are often based on English common law. The British Judicial Committee of the Privy Council still serves as the highest court of appeal for twelve former colonies.

Historians' approaches to understanding the British Empire are diverse and evolving. Two key sites of debate over recent decades have been the impact of post-colonial studies, which seek to critically re-evaluate the history of imperialism, and the continued relevance of historians Ronald Robinson and John Gallagher, whose work greatly influenced imperial historiography during the 1950s and 1960s. In addition, differing assessments of the empire's legacy remain relevant to debates over recent history and politics, such as the Anglo-American invasions of Iraq and Afghanistan, as well as Britain's role and identity in the contemporary world.

Historians such as Caroline Elkins have argued against perceptions of the British Empire as a primarily liberalising and modernising enterprise, criticising its widespread use of violence and emergency laws to maintain power. Common criticisms of the empire include the use of detention camps in its colonies, massacres of indigenous peoples, and famine-response policies. Some scholars, including Amartya Sen, assert that British policies worsened the famines in India that killed millions during British rule. Conversely, historians such as Niall Ferguson say that the economic and institutional development the British Empire brought resulted in a net benefit to its colonies. Other historians treat its legacy as varied and ambiguous. Public attitudes towards the empire within

Britain remain somewhat positive.

Printed by Libri Plureos GmbH in Hamburg, Germany